Social Media Marketing and Instagram Marketing

Take Your Business or Personal Brand Instagram Page to the Next Level with these Amazing Content Marketing Secrets - Instagram Advertising for Beginners

By

Michael Branding

Social Media Marketing and Instagram Marketing

Michael Branding

Published by Online Creative Services, 2021.

While every precaution has been taken in the preparation of this book, the publisher assumes no responsibility for errors or omissions, or for damages resulting from the use of the information contained herein.

SOCIAL MEDIA MARKETING AND INSTAGRAM MARKETING

First edition. January 19, 2021.

ISBN: 978-1393205012

Written by Michael Branding.

Chapter 1 - Basic Concepts

Social media marketing is a powerful way for businesses, professionals and organizations of all sizes to find and connect with returning or potential customers or users. Social marketers thus create company Facebook pages and accounts on Twitter, Instagram, Pinterest and other major social networks to reach this goal.

However, not all of these professionals really have clear goals and well defined strategies, nor an in-depth knowledge of how social media interact with consumers and how they can use this interaction to increase brand awareness, boost sales and profits, and create brand loyalty. This is why we strongly recommend that you understand how social media marketing actually works and deeply study the content of this book, as it has everything you need to know to turn your online presence into a money making machine.

Knowing the ABC of social media marketing, having understood exactly what social media marketing is, how it works, how much it requires in terms of time, human resources and budget, is the fundamental premise for those who want to do social marketing in a professional and effective way. This is why it is important to get started by having a clear and exhaustive definition of social media marketing. Knowing the field you are moving on is the best way to avoid big mistakes, especially at the beginning stages. Whether you want to build your personal brand or are looking for resources to boost your company presence online, you cannot skip this first important step.

So, let's get started.

Social media marketing or SMM (also known as social network marketing, social marketing, and, by extension, also facebook marketing, linkedin marketing, etc...) is a branch of online marketing applied to social networks. This discipline exploits the ability of social media and web-social applications (apps) to generate interaction (engagement) and social sharing, in order to increase the visibility and notoriety of a brand, a product or service, a freelancer or a public figure. It includes activities such as the promotion and sale of particular goods and services, the generation of new business contacts (which are called "leads") and the increase in traffic to a brand's official website or social pages.

For promotional purposes it is good to integrate a social media marketing strategy with other forms of online marketing, such as: Search Engine Marketing (SEM), Social Media Optimization (SMO), Social Media Advertising (SMA) or Social ads, and Public digital relations or Digital Pr.

Social media marketing, together with social customer service, social selling and other branches of digital marketing, is considered a component of Social Business, since it also includes pay-per-click marketing activities.

Companies and organizations create, or connect to, "networks of individuals" (communities) that share interests and values expressed by the company on social networks. Then, they use these online communities to offer their users relevant content in various formats (mainly text, images and videos) in order to stimulate discussions around the brand.

This is the concrete expression of a very important marketing principle: when people speak about a company, that company can take advantage of the attention, no matter what people say about the company.

In fact, if managed correctly, user and customer interaction with these contents can produce loyalty and social media advocacy. Users and customers, with their "likes", "comments" and "shares" activate word of mouth online by individually involving their network (friends, fans and followers) in the discussion. If you have a company, you know how powerful word of mouth is. Now imagine how big of an impact it can have on your business, when you take it online, where there is virtually no limit on the amount of people one single individual can enter in contact with.

This greatly increases the possibility that a percentage of them ends up becoming a fan or follower of the company or the brand.

An important distinction: Social marketing or social media marketing?

Sometimes on blogs, podcasts and other online content, social marketing is mistakenly used as a synonym for social media marketing. In reality, social marketing is a popular discipline that became famous in the early 1970s thanks to Philip Kotler and Gerald Zaltman. When we are talking about social marketing, the "product" to be promoted is not a good or a service but is "human behavior". The goal of a social advertising campaign is in fact, for example, to encourage people to protect the environment or to fight against racism.

It is just a simple distinction, but it is important to keep this in mind as in this book we are always referring to social media marketing, not social marketing.

Chapter 2 - Advantages and Disadvantages of Social Media Marketing

Now that we have discussed and understood the definition of social media marketing, let's try to understand what benefits it can bring to a company or a personal brand. Here is a list of the main reasons why social media marketing is one of the greatest tools available to anyone that wants to do business online.

- Improvement of customer satisfaction. It has been proven that clients that can get in contact with the brand behind their favourite product are more likely to report a positive shopping experience and become returning customers.

- Increase in customer loyalty (brand loyalty). As mentioned above, people that can see a powerful online presence tend to deem that brand as "solid" and "reliable", which inevitably translates to more money for the company.

- Customer service improvement. Having a good social media presence can help a brand to give a better customer service to its clients by answering their questions directly on the different platforms. Furthermore, this behaviour improves the reliability of the company and helps people that are on the fence to become paying customers.

- Increase in sales leads and sales. As we will see in the coming chapters, social media marketing can be used to actively increase the number of leads and sales, thanks to online advertising tools.

- Increase in web traffic to the company site or personal blog. This is easy to understand. When you attract the attention of someone, you can redirect that attention wherever you want. Your or your company website is a good choice in most cases.

● Better positioning of your sitei on search engines. This is closely connected with the previous point. When you direct the attention you attract on social media to a website, that website becomes more interesting for Google and other search engines. Therefore, it is not a surprise that social media marketing is also a great way to increase the organic reach of the brand website.

● Increase in brand awareness. This really needs no comment. Brand awareness, as we will see in the coming chapters, is extremely important in this day and age.

● Connection and development of interactive relationships with your target audience. Being able to engage with your target audience is truly an incredible gift, as it allows you to better understand your customers' needs and satisfy them with your amazing product or service.

● Development of a reputation as an expert or leader in the relevant sector (brand authority). By improving your social presence, you improve the view that the general public has of your brand. Think about Apple or Tesla: they have an amazing social presence and they are considered by everyone the leader in their sector.

But is it all sunshines and rainbows?

Well, that could not be farther from the truth. In fact, social media marketing also presents some difficulties to the newcomers, but they are all manageable with the right skills. Before diving deeper, we would like to point out some point of resistance that you or your brand may face when getting started.

● Lack of resources. Social networks are varied and different, consequently the various forms of content (text, video, podcast, webinar, etc.) that have to be published and shared must be adapted to the specificities of each one of them. Likewise, a social media marketing campaign cannot be launched and left alone. It requires time and human resources dedicated to it, in order to be profitable in the long run.

This is the reason why, at a certain point, especially for many small companies and personal brands, social media marketing becomes too expensive. By continuing reading this book you will understand how you can reduce the costs, while still building an impactful online presence.

● Negative feedback from your customers. When we discussed the advantages of social media marketing, we stated that word of mouth is an amazing tool to boost sales. Well, that is true if people are talking positively about you. The opposite effect comes when people start giving bad feedback. This can escalate quickly and can lead to a substantial loss of users or clients.

You can avoid this in many ways, but the best one is to have a truly amazing product.

Chapter 3 - The Importance of Social Media Marketing

So, we have now come to the most important question of them all. Why should a company or personal brand invest in social media marketing? Let's discuss some points together.

- Low costs. Creating profiles on social networks is free as well as creating and managing social media campaigns with your own social media management team.

- High ROI (return on investment) from advertising costs. The ROI generated by social media advertising is the highest among the various forms of paid advertising. Furthermore, social ads are a type of advertising that allows for high target profiling and personalization. This means that the ads will only be shown to users who are really interested in products or services promoted by the advertiser. This is crucial, as it allows you to cut out everyone that is not in target with what you are offering.

- High conversion rate (CR). More than 51% of social media marketers say that developing meaningful relationships with customers has a positive impact on sales results. This inevitably increases the conversion rate of advertising.

- Improvement of customer insights. Unlike content shared through private channels such as e-mails, instant messaging tools and apps, which are therefore difficult to measure, various social media marketing tools allow precise monitoring of activities on various social networks. From the analysis of the numerous data collected (insight) using tools such as Google Analytics, it is possible to obtain important information on the "sentiment" towards the brand, as well as on the demographic composition, interests, behaviors and needs of customers.

The importance of Social Media Marketing for businesses and personal brands

Why is social media marketing important? Social networks have become a virtual meeting place for people, where:

- they exchange ideas on the most disparate topics.

- they read reviews on products and services they want to buy.

- they look for information on places they want to go, such as restaurants or hotels.

Once, when these social platforms did not exist, this exchange of news took place in clubs or in other social gathering spaces. Today, however, people spend much more time on Instagram, Facebook, YouTube or LinkedIn and that is where they often "meet" and talk to each other. What does this mean? This means that companies and professionals should increasingly work on the ability to intercept and engage users in discussions on online social networks, because in these online environments it is possible to make them become their customers. People's opinions are increasingly influenced by conversations on the internet and this is a fact to take into account if you are selling a product on the web, if you are marketing online, or even if you just want to become important and relevant as an influencer.

Why does this trend affect us? If you are a businessman, or an online marketer, to reach your audience - which is your potential customer base - you must become good at getting noticed where they can find you. And by now you should have understood that that place is online. You must be present and be able to influence the opinions of those who have to make purchasing decisions and you have to do that online, because it is there that purchasing decisions are made more and more frequently.

Chapter 4 - Social Media Marketing as a Career

If you are not an entrepreneur that wants to take their company online, but you are just starting to look at social media marketing as a career opportunity, just know that being proficient on social media is also important for those looking for new professional opportunities. This will help you to:

- find a job in a fresh and up to date company;

- be desired by businesses all around the world. In fact, the internet has destroyed physical boundaries and companies look for talents from all around the world, thanks to the possibility given by smart working;

- have career opportunities and increasing earnings. You have to know that social media managers are paid very well, especially if they can provide concrete results to the company they are working for.

To be interesting and attractive to companies, it will also be appropriate to become good at handling the different software, tools and platforms through which you can reach users interested in a product or service on social networks.

Who is the social media marketer?

The Social media marketer (or social media manager) is a digital marketing professional who manages and supervises the social media, digital media and social network channels within a company and acts as a connection between a community of users and the company itself.

He is also responsible for designing the content strategy, managing social media marketing campaigns on Facebook, Twitter and other social networks with the help of the social media team; the creation of an editorial plan with a view to seo; the promotion of products, services and events, and sharing the contents of the company website or blog. In small and medium-sized businesses, the role of the social media marketer is delegated to figures usually subordinate to him such as:

- Web Content Editor
- Community Manager
- Social Media Specialist
- Digital Marketing Manager
- Digital PR Manager
- Social media strategist
- Facebook Ads Specialist
- Social Customer Care Specialist

Chapter 5 - Social Media Marketing in 7 Steps

There are various ways in which a company or organization can do social media marketing. However, all social media marketing activities carried out to be effective cannot be separated from the implementation of an effective social media marketing strategy. But how to define and set up a successful social media marketing strategy?

As in any digital marketing strategy, this is developed through the definition of a social media marketing plan which consists of some precise phases. Let's take a closer look at each one of them.

Please, note that this chapter serves a general structure for the key concept that will be discussed later on in the book.

Step 1 - Conducting a social media marketing audit

In this first step, the audit activity is aimed at evaluating the digital assets (blog, site, app, etc.) available, also in relation to the competition, in order to detect on each social channel what works and what does not work.

In order to simplify this process, here is a list of a few questions that you should aim to answer in this first step. Be as precise as possible, as it will dictate the fundamental aspects of your social media marketing strategy.

- On which social platforms is the brand currently active?

- Which social networks carry the most value?

- What kind of content do competitors post?

- What tone of voice did they choose?

- How much traffic to the website does each social channel bring?

- What types of content do we post on the different channels? How frequently?

- Are we getting results from investing in social media advertising?

Step 2 - Definition of your social media marketing goals

Having analyzed the digital assets, audience and competition, the next step in establishing an effective social media strategy concerns the definition of goals and results that you hope to achieve (number of leads, customer loyalty, increased sales, brand awareness, etc.)

These goals need to be aligned with the overall communication and marketing strategy so that social media enables the achievement of business goals. In setting goals, to ensure that these will be achieved, it is good to follow the SMART method (specific, measurable, feasible, realistic, as a function of time) used for the first time by Drucker in 1954, in the book "The practice of Management" .

Step 3 - Identification of your target audience

You need to be clear who your target audience is so that the message you want to convey on social media is effective. Developing typical customer profiles (buyer personas) is essential for the development of a social media marketing strategy. The collection and analysis of data on the web or from conducting online surveys allow the marketer to paint a well rounded profile of the typical customer. Once the audience has been defined, through surveying activities, they can understand on which social platforms the customer (real or potential) is present.

How do you define your target audience?

We have a dedicated chapter in this book, but let's get a simple idea in order to better understand phase 4.

The surveying activity can be carried out with the help of some social media monitoring tools for marketing automation or manually. Let's briefly see with this last method how to do surveying on Facebook, Twitter and LinkedIn:

1. Write down a list of keywords that are meaningful to you that indicate your product, service, brand or need that you can satisfy.
2. Enter the chosen keyword in the search field of the social network and wait for the results. In the search box you can filter them by "main results", "people", "pages", "places", "groups", "applications" and "events".
3. Enter the following data relating to the comments obtained (date, author, influence, sentiment) in an excel file and store it. This will give you an overview of what is being said online about the chosen brand or topic.

Step 4 - Creating a social media content strategy

Contents are very important in order to create engagement and to achieve your social media marketing goals. With this in mind, it is essential to follow a strategic approach focused on the creation and distribution of relevant and valuable content (Content Marketing), aimed at a clearly defined audience. This is why it is important to do step 3 before starting to produce content without a target audience in mind.

For the communication strategy on the various social media to be effective, however, it will be good to plan the management of these contents. This process is called content strategy and it requires an editorial plan.

For the planning of the editorial plan it can be useful to draw up a matrix of the contents or to use the 80/20 rule of Pareto. In the latter case, 80% of the posts must be used to inform, train or entertain their audience, while the remaining 20% to promote the brand. As for the frequency of publication, given that quality beats quantity, for a small company 2 or 3 weekly contents are generally sufficient. Here are some of the most popular types of content:

- Infographics
- Articles
- Images
- Videos
- Ebooks
- Interviews
- Institutional or corporate news announcements
- Live and virtual events
- Assistance (customer care)

Step 5: Pay attention to Influencers

Research carried out on Twitter shows that 49% of consumers rely on the advice of Influencers in making purchasing decisions. Finding those who have a large social following for recommendations on the products or services you sell is therefore very important for the success of your social media marketing strategy. One way for a company to gain visibility with social influencers is to use the sharing system suggested by Joe Pulizzi and the Content Marketing Institute, known as Social Media 4-1-1. For every 6 content shared via social media, 4 must be relevant content for your target audience but written by influencers; 1 must be original content created by us; 1 content must be about the sale of your product or service (a coupon for example). You can see how Joe Pulizzi agrees with the Pareto Principle as well.

To engage influencers, I invite you to also take into account any affiliate program to propose to those who are part of your niche. Affiliate marketing, in fact, provides for the payment of a commission to an intermediary, in this case the influencer, for each sale or lead that it manages to generate among its audience. This translates into a win-win situation. The influencer is happy because he can get a portion of the revenues generated and the company is happy because it can get sales without spending money.

Step 6 - Choosing the social media marketing platform

A social media marketing strategy must also be planned taking into account the market in which the company operates (B2B or B2C), the purchasing decision-making phase (social consumer decision journey) in which the customer may possibly be found (research, consideration, decision). Knowing the differences between the platforms and identifying the best ones to support the company's marketing objectives is fundamental. So let's take a brief look at the most famous social networks, not focusing on what these social media are, but in relation to the marketing activities that can be implemented with them.

Facebook

With almost 2.1 billion users and a growth of 15% (year-on-year figure), it is one of the largest social networks in the world. With this social platform it is possible to precisely identify your target audience, create engagement starting from Facebook Groups, easily implement real alternative advertising campaigns to Adwords. The possibility of integrating content in various formats into Facebook is endless and recently it is also possible by clicking on a special button to integrate Instagram content. Users of MailChimp, an email marketing software, can then natively create Facebook ads from their account.

Facebook has many arrows in its bow (Facebook media, Facebook business manager, Facebook live, Facebook connect, Facebook Stories, Facebook news feed ads, Facebook video ads). Let's briefly see the characteristics of some of them:

- Facebook Ads. Advertising on Facebook allows you to reach a conversion rate of 30% higher than other social platforms and allows a decrease in costs per conversion of 50%

- Facebook Places. Is the Facebook geo-location service that allows the user to add information about the place where he is, and based on this, find places, information of interest divided by category (restaurants, shops, entertainment, etc.) and friends who are nearby.

The presence of "tiles" or boxes that refer to company fan pages make it a valuable tool for social media marketing activities.

● Facebook media. It is a tool used to teach users who have created fan pages on Facebook to manage them effectively. To access Facebook media just connect to media.fb.com.

● Facebook bluetooth beacons. The social network provides devices applicable to a physical area of your business (beacons) that allow you to send marketing communications (promotional offers, etc.) via smartphone to potential customers who pass in your vicinity. To request beacons, you must register on their waiting list.

● Facebook business manager. Is a free and easy to use tool for advertising and marketing on Facebook. From its dashboard it is possible to monitor the performance of anything connected to your business on Facebook.

Another particularity offered by Facebook is the possibility given to marketers to create effective advertising campaigns aimed at a relatively small audience through Dark Marketing activities. Through a Chrome app (Power Editor) it is possible to create "dark posts" on Facebook. In short, Facebook gives advertisers the ability to create sponsored posts that do not appear on the user's timeline but are accessible to anyone with a direct link or by clicking from an ad.

Instagram

Instagram is a photo sharing application for iPhone, Android and Windows platforms. At the heart of Instagram social media marketing are Instagram stories. They are a way to share photos and videos with your followers that will no longer be visible after 24 hours. Instagram lends itself a lot to social web marketing: people post images and videos, tag friends, insert hashtags and click on content shared by others, making Instagram the social network with the highest engagement rate.

On Instagram it is also possible to post a new type of post called "shoppable post" which includes a special tag that connects the objects in the photo directly to the corresponding e-commerce. Instagram is now testing a new "nametags" feature similar to Snapchat's Snapcodes or Messenger code that makes it easier to acquire Instagram followers. Its "visual" features make this social network suitable for b2b social media marketing, such as travel business, e-commerce and social events.

LinkedIn

LinkedIn is one of the best professional social platforms to connect with your network of collaborators (Linkedin groups) and potential future employers. The social network allows users to import contacts and integrates services such as SlideShare and Pulse. Today LinkedIn is the most popular social network for professionals in the world and is considered the most effective B2B social media marketing and lead generation platform. Like other social platforms, also on Linkedin it is possible to manage advertisements (Linkedin ads). The platform also offers businesses and publishers the ability to natively run video ad campaigns and include videos within their company pages. Through the implemented Linkedin Tracking pixel, it is then possible to measure the number of leads, sign-ups, visits to websites and other actions generated by video ads.

Snapchat

Snapchat is a mobile application that allows users to send photos and videos to friends. Snapchat Stories (collages of photos and videos shared for no more than 24 hours) are a great engagement tool. With the release of the new version of the app, it will soon be possible to share Snapchat stories also on Facebook and Twitter. Snapchat is testing new in-app e-commerce options through its Snap store located within the Discover platform, which could lead to partnerships with companies of all kinds in the future. If your products are aimed at a very young audience, marketing on Snapchat is definitely the right choice.

Pinterest

Pinterest is a popular photo sharing service that allows anyone to create collections and more. 93% of its users use it to plan purchases or to research product information. Marketing activities are possible thanks to Pinterest ads and buyable pins. Pinterest is continuing to grow among small and medium enterprises. The adhesions to its Pinterest Propel program in fact recorded a + 50% this year. With 81% of its 150 million monthly active users being women, topics such as interior design, decoration, cooking and clothing work very well.

Reddit

Reddit is the social network where the community decides what will be more relevant and what to give more visibility to. Reddit has a subreddit (think of it as a digital board) for almost every category. The growth of this social network in the world is due to 2 factors: the AMAs format (ask me everything) and the peculiarities of the voting system. Marketing activities are possible thanks to Reddit ads, however, it is necessary to pay close attention to the large number of comments received and therefore it requires constant attention.

Telegram

Telegram is a messaging application that allows you to chat with contacts, organizing public and private groups, with a series of functions dedicated to visual content. You can add images, emojis, documents, files and links to messages. Companies can use Telegram to notify their clients of new offers and promotions or to directly chat with them if we are talking about a small and close community.

Tumblr

Tumblr is a microblogging platform with social networking features. Much used by fashion brands, bloggers and designers for the publication of very accurate content. People spend more time on this platform than on Facebook, which makes Tumblr a good place to post and advertise.

Twitter

Twitter is another fantastic social media platform that allows users to quickly send 280-character posts through Tweets. These are characterized by the presence in the text of an hashtag (a keyword preceded by the hash symbol #). Twitter marketing is often used by companies to maintain contact with their customers, to promote their brands, products or services, and to obtain information from consumers.

Whatsapp

Whatsapp is one of the most used instant messaging applications in the world given the ease of use and quality of service. In 2017 WhatsApp crossed the milestone of 1 billion users per day, thus equaling Facebook. The app offers the possibility of interacting with your contacts within conversations and today you can publish, as status updates, temporary Snapchat-style photos and videos. With the release this year of WhatsApp Business, and the coming integration of the possibility of making payment, the brand officially accesses one-to-one marketing.

Disqus

Disqus was born as a commentary hosting service for websites and blogs. This platform now represents a real social network where users can give life to debates or participate in existing ones. To manage comments, just access the platform with the same account used for social media, using the "share" button you can then bring the discussion to your favorite social network.

YouTube

Youtube is a network where users post video blogs, video ads and videos of various genres. For marketers, videos are the ideal medium to share medium to long-form content and Youtube is the go to hosting place for video content.

Step 7 - Measurement and testing

It is necessary to constantly analyze the social media marketing strategies implemented to understand which has been effective and which has not. As part of a social media marketing strategy, it is necessary to decide which metrics or KPIs to use to verify whether the set goals have been achieved. Some metrics to consider to measure the success of a social media marketing strategy are the following:

- Cost per click (CPA)
- Conversion Rate
- Number of followers
- Brand mention
- Total shares
- Impressions
- Comments and engagement

Chapter 6 - Social Media Marketing Trends for 2021

Social media are dynamic by their nature and, for this reason, they are characterized by trends and communication methods that can vary over time (ever heard about social media trends). Knowing these trends can be crucial in choosing the most direct and effective social media marketing strategies. Below is a brief description of the social media marketing strategies that, as it seems, will most characterize 2021.

1. Use Tik Tok for your Social Media Marketing strategy. This social network is growing rapidly and is a must for those who want to reach users under 30, which currently represents 66% of the channel's users.

2. Social media wellness becomes essential to create engagement among users. People are gaining greater awareness of the use of social networks and the impact they have on mental health. This is why even the platforms themselves are committed to making the user experience pleasant and not very harmful. If you notice changes in the level of engagement, you should not be scared, but observe your competitors and if they suffer the same reduction you can feel comfortable. People are increasingly trying to reduce their time on social media and leverage the time they spend constructively.

3. Fake news will be limited. This is certainly excellent news and a very positive trend. The fact that fake news is on the decline does not mean that it still does not remain a problem. For those involved in social media marketing this means that the user will weigh heavily what you declare about your company and your products. So, please, maximum transparency!

4. Tightened security. Another growing trend strongly correlated to social media marketing is user security. The recent scandal involving Facebook and Cambridge Analytica is likely to further enhance this trend. The privacy protection measures for users of Social networks will have to be increasingly suitable to fight hacking, identity theft, phishing and various other security threats.

5. A more effective strategy with augmented reality and virtual reality. Technology is taking great steps towards AR and VR and you must be able to adapt to this change. Augmented reality and virtual reality will improve not only the effectiveness of your strategy, but also the experience of your users.

6. The use of artificial intelligence will increase. The use of artificial intelligence (chatbots and virtual assistants) will increasingly allow marketers to interact with consumers in real time and in a personalized way. Facebook is preparing to relaunch a virtual assistant that will be able to offer suggestions to users and answer all their requests through the Facebook Messenger chat. According to Gartner, a world-leading multinational company in strategy consulting, research and analysis in the field of Information Technology (IT), 20% of business content could be generated this year by machines similar to artificial intelligence. Think about it, of every ten articles you read online, two of them are probably written by a robot.

7. Designing the social media marketing strategy to involve Generation Z. The generation of the future is becoming more and more involved with technology and this requires innovation and creativity from marketers. 2021 will be the year of the challenge to find new ways to entertain and involve the youngest, studying them carefully and understanding their needs.

8. Influencer Marketing. Social media influencers are able to generate a return on investment 11 times greater than any other digital marketing strategy. It is no coincidence that 94% of social media marketers claim to have achieved excellent results thanks to their collaboration and consider them an integral part of their social media marketing strategy.

In recent years, this tactic has been used in many sectors (social media marketing for tourism is an example above all), with results such as to become the main digital channel for many companies. The success and evolution of this tactic has also favored the creation of numerous new professional figures. Among the most sought after we find the social media marketer.

Chapter 7 - SMART Method for Goal Setting

Here is a quick overview of the SMART method.

Specific, measurable, attainable, realistic and time effective: this is how goals should be formulated, so that they are effective for the purposes of our planning and organization work. Use the SMART method for formulating goals. In this way, all the criteria that a well-formulated goal must possess will be respected.

The aim is to create an exceptional planning and organization process. Knowing what we want to achieve with our social media marketing strategy is important, but how do we state that clearly so that we can increase the odds of actually achieving our goals?

This is where the SMART method comes into place. As mentioned before, SMART is an acronym and indicates the criteria for the formulation of a goal, which must therefore be specific, measurable, attainable, realistic and have a specific time period.

Specific goals

We often make the first mistake by not reflecting deeply on what we want to achieve with our social media marketing strategy and we favor an inadequately specific formulation of our goals.

Examples of non-specific objectives:

"We want to make more money."

"We want more followers."

What do these statements mean? When is it "in the future"? And how much would you like to increase the number of followers? What does it mean to make more money? Does it refer to sales or profit? Neither objective specifies what the final perspective is. Take this into account when formulating your goal.

The same goals formulated specifically:

"In the next month, we want to increase our monthly revenue by 5% using social media marketing"

"In the next month, we will get at least 1000 more followers on our Instagram page."

Measurable goals

In order to verify the achievement of the goal or to get motivated to work towards it, the goal must be measurable.

Examples of non-measurable goals:

"We want to post beautiful images on our social media pages."

"We want to have good comments on our posts."

What does beautiful images mean? When do you deem a comment as good? Do not leave room for interpretation. Formulate the goal in such a way that it can be verified whether it has been achieved or not.

Examples of measurable goals:

"We want to post images on social media pages that get at least 1000 likes."

"We want to receive one positive feedback every two customers."

Attainable goals

In order not to give up on your goals, it is necessary that you recognize them as such and accept it. In other words: the goal must be attractive to your or your company eyes.

Examples of unattainable goals:

"During the week we will post 100 times per day."

"In the future, all customer inquiries will be dealt with immediately."

Be honest with yourself. Can you accept these goals? Will they be attractive enough to your eyes even over a period of months? Set goals in such a way that for you personally and for all employees they are actually achievable and remain attractive over time.

Examples of attainable goals:

"We dedicate myself to our social channels consistently, posting at least 5 times per day to create brand awareness."

"All customer inquiries will be processed within 48 hours."

Realistic goals

In the throes of ambition, we have the feeling of being able to achieve anything. But even then, be honest with yourself. Are you able and are you willing to achieve these goals and keep chipping at them?

Examples of unrealistic goals:

"At the end of the day we always respond to all the comments we received that day."

"From now on we will always refund our customers."

Don't be fooled by your ambition when formulating goals. Stay realistic to avoid bankruptcy in the short term.

Examples of realistic goals:

"We organize our comment according to priorities (1 = urgent / 2 = to be fulfilled within 2 days / 3 = to be fulfilled by the end of the week) and we make sure that at the end of the day we have carried out the tasks of priority 1."

"We will refund customers that actually are suitable for the refund, based on the contract they signed when they made the purchase."

Time effective goals

Don't leave the deadline of your goal to chance.

Examples of non time effective goals:

"We will post on our social channels."

"We will answer those comments."

You now have unlimited time to do those two things. Sooner or later these goals will be reached. However, you prefer to define in the goal itself the deadline by which you want to reach it or put it into practice:

Examples of time effective goals:

"We will post on our social channels by 9am every day."

"We will answer those comments before lunch."

Think about the SMART method the next time you formulate goals for your social media marketing strategy and write them down. In this way it will be easier for you not to lose sight of them and to achieve them faster.

Chapter 8 - Pareto Principle and the Yerkes and Dodson Curve

The Pareto principle is also called the "80/20 law" or the "Pareto effect". Regardless of how you decide to call it, the principle is named after its discoverer Vilfredo Pareto (1848-1923). At the beginning of the 20th century, Pareto, an engineer, sociologist and economist, conducted research concerning the subdivision of popular heritage in Italy. Pareto's research showed that one fifth, or 20% of Italian citizens, had about 80% of the national wealth.

Pareto therefore deduced that the banks should have concentrated on that 20% of Italians to be more efficient and obtain greater profits, thus indirectly establishing that the banks only devote a fifth of their time to assisting the remaining 80% of the population.

The Pareto principle represented the inequality of the division and the lack of balance between the resources used and profit. However, this proportion was also true in other sectors.

- Commerce: 20% of products or customers invoice 80% of earnings.
- Storage: 20% of products take up 80% of the places on the shelves.
- Internet: 80% of data traffic is generated on 20% of websites.
- Road transport: 80% of all journeys take place on 20% of roads.
- Phone calls: 80% of calls are made to and from 20% of the saved contacts

The 80/20 law is best known for its application in time management. Because with a correct setting of your time it is possible to do 80% of the work in 20% of the time taken.

The goal of the rule discovered by Pareto is to achieve the greatest result with the least effort, since a lot of time is often invested in tasks with lower priority. With the right priorities and better time management, however, you can set up your work more efficiently and in a targeted manner. The Pareto principle is particularly suitable for those professional sectors with tight deadlines, allowing you to focus your efforts in the most efficient way possible and to complete the tasks within the established time frame. This 80/20 law is usually associated with other methods of time management, such as the Eisenhower principle.

There are some types of errors that are often encountered in the application of the principle in question. The first is that it is wrongly claimed that with 20% of the time invested, 80% more than normal is reached, thus bringing the yield to 100%. This is clearly a misinterpretation, where the figures are added together, thus leading to 100%, despite the fact that they are actually two different and separate aspects. Commitment and performance are not the same thing and therefore cannot be added together so easily. To generate 100% of the yield you need to commit 100% and that is especially true when it comes to social media marketing.

An interpretation of this type serves no other purpose than to give false hopes, which are far too optimistic. However, understanding the functioning of the basic principle is not enough to avoid misinterpreting its use. In fact, one might be led to think, always wrongly, that it is enough to reduce all tasks to only 20%. But here too, we must not get confused: many of the jobs that need to be done in social media marketing do not lead directly to the goal, however they are necessary to get there. Writing and replying to emails fall within the duties of this type, which in fact, although they may seem a negligible element and of little relevance to the success of a company, are nevertheless essential.

The Pareto principle serves precisely to optimize those tasks that remain necessary despite generating less or no profit, so as to take away as little time as possible. Any incorrect use of the Pareto principle can lead to the attribution of too low importance to a large part of the work to be carried out. The fact is that only those who dedicate themselves to their work in a conscious, concentrated and structured manner can obtain 80% of the results with 20% of the work done. Social media marketing falls perfectly under this principle.

The 80/20 law is very versatile. It can be used in one's private life, in study and at work for better time management. In our case, we use it to develop a much more effective and time saving social media marketing strategy. The important thing is to know which activity contributes most to achieving what you want, so as to be able to give the right priority to the various tasks. The Pareto principle helps to make the best choice in this regard.

From a purely theoretical point of view, the Pareto principle can be applied in any sector, not only in social media marketing. It has seen successful application in school and academic training, as well as in everyday life for normal people. Often the 80/20 law is associated with the working life, where it is more usual to have strict deadlines and well defined goals. But even in everyday private life there are many tasks that must be carried out in a short time and as efficiently as possible.

An example for everyday life

In order to understand the importance of Pareto Principle for social media marketing optimization, it can be useful to take a look at a common everyday life scenario.

If friends or family tell you that they will be visiting you shortly, there is little time left to clean up the house. Normally, to put everything in order and carry out all the household chores, it usually takes three hours, but in the case of such a visit, it often takes no more than an hour and a half. For this reason, following what is determined by the Pareto principle, it is initially advisable to focus on those that contribute to the well-being of the guests. Collecting objects and clothes around the apartment, putting dirty dishes in the dishwasher and cleaning the table is part of these chores.

The rooms most often used by guests are the living room, bathroom and dining room, and are therefore the ones on which you need to focus initially. Cleaning these rooms practically corresponds to the aforementioned 80% of "success", while one's bedroom, cellar and the like alter the mood of guests to a lesser extent.

In social media marketing this translates, for instance, into taking care of the most important customer requests first, prioritizing them over the less urgent ones.

Yerkes and Dodson curve

Similarly to the Pareto principle, Yerkes and Dodson law also has to do with the relationship between commitment and productivity. The curve in question takes its name from psychologists Robert Yerkes and John Dodson. From their research it emerged that productivity improves proportionally according to the growth of the commitment, at least until the maximum point is reached, or the point where the improvement in performance reaches its maximum, thus leading to a decrease in productivity.

The Yerkes and Dodson curve is represented by an inverted U. Despite continuing to invest time and energy, productivity inevitably begins to decline once the top is reached. The high pressure and the resulting stress cause a decrease in performance, leading to worse results. Like the Pareto Principle, the Yerkes and Dodson law also affirms, or rather confirms, that only a certain part of the commitment leads to most of the productivity. The remaining effort required to achieve 100% results leads to very little in terms of productivity.

Chapter 9 - Identify the Correct Buyer Persona

As for every concept we introduce in this book, let's start by giving a detailed definition of what a buyer persona is and what it is not.

Buyer personas are fictitious representations of typical customers of a company, created on the basis of data collected through surveys or interviews, taking into account not only their socio-demographic, psychographic and behavioral characteristics but also data, quotes and sayings that can be useful for creating ad hoc products and services.

These are archetypes or models that result from insights provided by consumers and users. Making use of buyer personas therefore means starting from the study of real customers to guide business and marketing strategies that will lead to the involvement, conversion and loyalty of new buyers. The insights collected may concern various types of data, such as personal information, expressions used, ways of speaking and quotes, taken during interviews, which allow us to illustrate in a more "human" way, thus going beyond the numbers and statistics relating to purchases and preferences, the "type" of person who visits a site, page or shop.

All the information collected and analyzed makes it possible to create archetypes from which brands can align their marketing strategy and brand positioning based, therefore, on the expectations of current customers and potential buyers.

The identification of buyer personas includes the collection and analysis of socio-demographic data, data relating to purchasing habits, payment methods, and much more. These are in fact useful information but not exhaustive if you intend to accurately identify the customer or the typical user of a business. As many expert explain, very often when we try to identify the target we mainly think about a demographic target. Maybe we think about the gender, the age group, the geographical area which our users come from. The reality of the facts is that what works in terms of communication is not so much knowing this information but what the behavioral and motivational data of the macro-groups and segments of users who arrive on our site are.

Knowing what their problems are and how they would like to solve them is useful, as it allows us to collect data relating to the value system of users or customers in order to create targeted content that meets their way of thinking and to conceive of reality.

The use of the term personas, intended as the creation of typical profiles of users who visit a website, is attributed to Alan Cooper, software designer and programmer who, thanks to his experience in the field, has developed and studied over the years the application of this methodology to the design sector for the creation of user-friendly software. The result of these researches was initially published in 1998 in "The Inmates Are Running the Asylum", a book that introduced the concept which then spread widely in various sectors.

The reason behind the construction of a buyer persona

These profiles are useful for guiding the decision-making process relating to multiple aspects of the business, such as the creation and definition of the characteristics of products, services and store, the definition of the structure and layout of a site, as well as marketing strategies. Furthermore, they help identify the correct brand positioning to be adopted to communicate our services and products in an appropriate manner to the various customer groups.

The traditional approach of identifying the target of a product, service or message is based on the collection of mainly quantitative data, obtained thanks to statistical analysis and socio-demographic information, but also related to purchasing behavior and preferences by channel communication.

However, this type of survey is not enough to identify the psychological nuances of the average customer or user of a site, as many marketing experts have explained during the years. In fact, as the expert explains, even if the definition of the target is essential to understand what to focus the company resources on and to identify the aspects of the business that need to be optimized, this only allows to clarify " what" to propose, but not "how" to offer it to customers. In fact, in planning a marketing strategy it is necessary to create content aimed at the different targets of the business, since a generalist and not very personalized communication cannot be in line with the way of communicating and reasoning of different customers and, therefore, it will be difficult to respond. to different doubts, worries and needs.

To better understand your target and create content that is truly relevant to potential customers, it is advisable to think like them and try to identify with the different buyer personas and their "thought structures" as David Meerman Scott explains in the aforementioned book. In the same book, the author explained that "the idea behind the concept of buyer personas is to understand your target so well that you practically start to think like him".

Design the perfect buyer persona for your company

The creation of these archetypes allows us to understand who the customers or users of a site are, but also the way they think, what they want to achieve and what are the objectives and reasons that guide their behavior, in addition to the methods and timing of purchase. To construct the identikit of the ideal customer or user, it is necessary to take into account different types of information relating to consumers and proceed with the collection of data through survey tools that allow you to listen to customers and then, in a subsequent phase, process the data that will allow to identify and construct the different buyer personas in an accurate and detailed way.

What data to collect

In the collection of data for the construction of the representations of the customer or the ideal user of a site, we range from the most personal information (such as socio-demographic, psychographic data, etc.) to those that instead relate more specifically to any response, approach or preference of the typical customer towards a product, a site or a company.

Socio-demographic data

Socio-demographic data allow you to "empathize" with buyer personas, giving them a human form, a face and an identity. Therefore, we are talking about information such as age, sex, origin, level of education, employment and income, as well as data relating to marital status, the number of children and the family unit. It is no coincidence, then, that Meerman Scott recommends giving a name to the buyer personas, precisely because these types of data allow you to "humanize" your company and related marketing strategies. Establishing that, for example, we must turn to Jane, a 37-year-old woman from New York, with more than one child and happily married, is useful to make the image that professionals have of a specific target group less abstract. This will simplify and identify the correct way they must address the communication of the brand or product.

In some cases, it may also be crucial to know the skills of the customer or typical user of our site. For example, the development of the design of a site or software or the versions of a site in different languages may vary depending on the target who in fact may be particularly familiar with those tools or may instead be a beginner. The same thing is true for linguistic skills. You have to ask yourself if a specific target group on the site knows the English language or if it is necessary to create a version in other languages as well. This, in particular, is something to be taken into consideration very seriously, especially in this multiethnic world.

Psychographic data

To understand how a certain type of customer thinks, it is also necessary to carry out a psychographic analysis, taking up elements that make it possible to identify some personality traits, attitudes, ways of thinking and typical saying of a particular buyer persona. For example, it would be appropriate to understand if it is more or less extroverted, if it is impulsive (which can affect the type of purchases and the impact of advertising communications), if it is particularly emotional or more rational, if it is more or less tending to savings, etc.

In addition to the preponderant character traits, we must also ask ourselves what fears, anxieties or frustrations can be. Think of a company that produces toys and the importance of identifying the greatest concerns of parents for their children. This, however, is not enough because it is useful to understand what leads them to buy that product. For example, parents could aim to buy a more "educational" toy, asking for opinions in the store or doing online searches, while grandparents could aim to please the child, deciding to buy a toy advertised in a TV commercial, perhaps even more expensive but which can satisfy the grandson's requests. This information can be useful in making decisions regarding the characteristics of the product, the price, but also the tone of voice of the advertising messages, therefore depending on the buyer persona to whom it is addressed.

Another important aspect concerns the predominant system of values for each buyer persona, that is, what are the moral principles not to be infringed, what kind of communication or marketing action could go against the ethical principles of a specific type of consumer. In this regard, as many experts explained over the years, it is necessary to identify the values that our brand or our site must keep alive in order not to go against the moral values of the users to whom it is approaching. Why? because, if on the one hand we are quite inclined and available to a change of opinion on certain ideas or concepts when someone (such as a brand) tries to convince us of something, on the other hand there are certain principles or values to which we are not willing to give up. One thing is certain values do not change and, on the contrary, we feel a sense of disgust and anger towards those who try to transmit moral values that are different from ours. Discover the value of your ideal customers and build your social media marketing strategy on them.

Furthermore, it is necessary to take into account not only the values but also any prejudices or preconceptions, conventions and opinions that people have regarding the most varied topics that can in some way interfere with the evaluation of a product or an advertisement and must be identified. and taken into consideration.

Needs, motivations and objectives of the buyer personas

Knowing the motivations, priorities and needs that lead customers to seek a specific solution, to solve a problem, to find out about the different brands that offer a certain service or to buy a certain product is essential to know what to focus economic efforts on identify the elements or characteristics to be highlighted in the communication of a product or brand.

On Alan Cooper's website, Kim Goodwin mentions the different types of objectives or expectations of the buyer persona that should be identified and which must affect the design of sites, products and planning of marketing strategies. The expert refers above all to life goals, such as retiring at 45. This particular goal may not be of great relevance to anyone designing a phone, but it may be useful for someone who is creating a financial planning tool.

Limits, problems and barriers to purchase

Another important element to analyze in detail is the perception that customers have of the brand or its products. Knowing the preconceptions, opinions and criticisms that consumers have to move to a given solution will allow brands to respond accordingly, proposing changes based on the various problems identified. Furthermore, once any obstacles to purchase have been identified, that is, anything that could lead a customer to decide that they no longer want to buy the product or even try it, companies can create a communication that allows them to overcome these obstacles.

Decision criteria

What criteria do different customers or users focus on for purchasing decisions? Knowing what drives consumers to choose one brand to the detriment of another is of great importance for companies, since it allows you to understand not only what the advantages that make your product essential for a specific target are, but also the problems that make it so that it prefers the solution offered by a competitor.

Buyer journey

The analysis of the buyer journey is essential first of all to understand which are the points of contact with the company that will allow you to reach the customer effectively, inspiring trust and meeting the preferences for the use of content and research of the information. It is necessary to know the process or the path taken by customers before arriving at the purchase of the product, so as to understand what difficulties or problems there are and how to overcome them effectively.

It is therefore of great interest to obtain data on all the obstacles that can intervene in the purchase process. How can you do this? For example, you can achieve this by asking the user the type of sources they use when looking for information on products or services and through which channels they usually receive or would prefer to receive commercial communications. Remember, if you control the journey of your customer you control your customer.

Effective tools for data collection

There are several tools that allow you to collect the information needed to build buyer personas. Social media, and therefore tools such as Facebook Audience Insights but also Google Analytics, can be very useful for collecting large amounts of demographic data, as well as the times in which each group of users is most active on the web, their geographical origin and related interests.

In addition to the processing of statistical data relating to personal data or purchasing behavior, the carrying out of interviews is particularly important because it also allows you to analyze the type of language used by the buyer personas and therefore understand the style of communication, the words, the terms that may hit them more. Therefore, it may be useful to extract from these one or more representative quotes of each buyer persona, their motivations, fears, aspirations, expectations towards brands or products but also their life goals, for example. On the basis of this information, short bibliographic descriptions can be constructed that can serve as inspiration for the creation of content aimed at that specific group of customers. You can also use online surveys sent via email through, for example, Google Form.

How to analyze the data you collect

Once the data has been collected, how to put them together to create the identities of the ideal customer or the different types of customers? As for the ideal number of buyer personas, according to David Meerman Scott, it must be identified "on the basis of the factors that differentiate them".

For example, some companies may have a different profile to represent the Asian, European and North American customer, thus creating different archetypes according to the different geographical areas in which it operates. It all depends on the sector, the type of company and business you offer, as well as the different target groups involved.

Chapter 10 - Content Strategy: Everything You Need to Know

Content strategy and content marketing are often confused and used as synonyms, but they are and remain well-defined elements with the first being hierarchically superior to the second. In fact, we will see how a content strategy can exist without even a glimpse of content marketing. Because "content is king" remains a valid dogma, but there is no king without a kingdom that has precise borders within which to exercise its hegemony.

Before diving deeper into content marketing, it is important to give a definition of what we are talking about and distinguish content marketing from content strategy.

Content marketing - definition

Content marketing is the creation and dissemination of useful and valuable content, aimed at a well-defined audience, with the aim of attracting it, acquiring it and inducing potential customers to take profitable actions.

Content strategy - definition

Content strategy deals with the planning aspects of content management throughout its life cycle. It includes the analysis phase, the alignment of the content with the business goals, influencing its development, production, presentation, evaluation, measurement and archiving. What the content strategy is not, however, is the content implementation phase. Practical development, management and dissemination of content are the tactical results of the strategy, what needs to be done for the strategy to be effective.

Thus, Rahel Anne Bailie, a famous content strategis, in an article on her blog dated 2009 but still valuable, stated this exact difference.

Basically, the two phases are split. The first one involves strategic planning and the second one, which is subsequent and regulated by the first, involves the creation and share of the content in its different forms.

Content strategy is what lies upstream, it is the planning activity that defines and regulates this process. The difference lies in the fact that the content strategist does not deal with the production of content but turns his attention to the planning of the same, not limiting himself to defining when they should be published but above all why they should be produced. Each content, in fact, must be a single brick useful to build the bigger building. It is a work of engineering and architecture for which not only workers and concrete are needed, but first of all a clear, defined project divided into several phases. Without precise planning, clear goals to strive for and measurable objectives to be achieved, the contents will be ineffective and self-referential. They simply won't "stand up", exactly like a building built in the absence of a blueprint.

Content strategy and content curation

As evidence of how much and how the content strategy has an absolute value greater than content marketing, there are numerous examples of strategies of extraordinary success without even the production of their own content. In this case, we leverage on content curation (defined as the ability to filter and add value to the contents we receive daily from all online sources, i.e. the process of selection, collection, organization and subsequent sharing of content relating to a particular topic or subject area).

We can offer useful content to potential customers that are simultaneously in line with our business goals. We are referring to reporting, commenting and rewriting articles written by third parties that thus enter the information sphere of our audience. In this way, we will add a valuable contribution capable of underlining our expertise in the field, the relevance of the subject for our industry and the usefulness of that information for those who receive it.

Structuring a winning content strategy

In a broader marketing action, whether it is inbound marketing or social media marketing, content remains the main focus or at least it should. In defining the strategy, a good content strategist can and must make use of numerous tools and suggestions to identify topics of interest. Among these, in addition to what a paid platform like Hubspot offers, Google offers valuable and free help. Through the Adwords keyword planner it is possible to know the search volume for the keyword that has been identified as being of interest for the target audience. Google Trends, on the other hand, allows you to measure the degree of interest of that keyword in a given period, thus knowing its variations, noticing any new trends.

However, the choice of specific topics to be treated is a step subsequent to numerous others that precede it. It will be essential to first establish what the goals of our marketing action are and which target we would like to talk to. Subsequently it will be necessary to identify a message that differentiates us from the competition and that can be the beacon of our communication. Then, thoroughly analyze the market and competitors and identify the most suitable channels to spread our messages. Finally, establish what KPIs to measure to be aware of the progress of our strategy.

Defining the goals for your content strategy in the most effective way

A content strategist is called upon to confront the objectives indicated by the companies for which he works. Often, these milestones are rather vague, complicated to quantify.

"I would like to have more visibility". Would it mean having more visitors to your site? Or, "I would like to increase sales". Ok, but on which segments? Not having a magic strategy that works for everything, you need to choose which categories of people to focus your communication on to try to increase sales in that specific area. It is therefore necessary to discuss and define the goals in advance in a precise and specific way. It is on the basis of them, moreover, that each individual content and the entire content strategy must be oriented.

For example, "increasing sales generated from the youngest portion of our clients" could be a clear, concrete, measurable goal and referred to a specific target.

But what are the most common goals that a content strategy can aim to achieve? Here is an exhaustive list, that will give you a better idea on where to focus your attention.

• **Lead generation.** Contents and landing pages structured in such a way as to facilitate the compilation of a form through which to obtain useful information on potential customers.

• **Media and digital pr.** Our goal will be to obtain media coverage by creating news that has an organic, viral diffusion.

• **Distinctive positioning**. Our purpose will be defined by communicating what exactly the company does, positioning it precisely in that sector and distinguishing it from its competitors. This is an extremely important goal that, if achieved can lead to enormous amount of success.

• **Customer support.** Our contents will be aimed at clarifying the terms and conditions of the service, the characteristics of the products and the sales mechanisms.

- **Community building.** Our editorial plan will be aimed at creating a sense of belonging, identification towards the brand through a sharing of values that emerges from a story that is as shared as possible, horizontal, friendly.

The definition of the target of a content strategy: the buyer persona

As discussed in the previous chapter, identifying the correct buyer persona is extremely important in a social media marketing strategy.

Mapping the purchasing process and intervening at every stage with the right content, at the right time, aimed at the right person is the overall and final goal of a well rounded content strategy.

To understand if a message is interesting or not, if a content can be relevant or not, we will have to understand who should receive it. Have in mind who to turn to at every time, as this is a crucial part of every social media marketing strategy.

Identifying your audience, defining it as specifically as possible is the key to drawing up a winning content strategy. Information such as age, gender, educational qualification, for many product categories are now superfluous.

At all levels of marketing, a fall in the importance of personal data is being observed in favor of buyer personas. The modern identity of the potential customer we address is reconstructed by integrating demographic and, above all, psychographic data. This means taking into strong consideration interests, behaviors, reasons for purchasing, doubts and fears regarding our service, product or our entire industry.

In short, information that is not only useful but essential to understand in which contexts these categories of people are more accessible and inclined to listen to our message and what makes that message relevant for them. We will have a dedicated chapter on this topic later on in this book.

Identify the differential message of the content strategy

Differentiate to qualify, that is key. A winning content strategy cannot ignore the identification of a differential message, of a corporate plus value that allows us to stand out from the competition. Our differential message will be our beacon. In fact, in all our content we will have to ask ourselves if it has been underlined, or at least implied. And it must be one and only one. The customer is bombarded with numerous advertisements every time he logs in and is looking for someone who can simplify his choice by clarifying which is the best, or most immediate, for that need he wants to satisfy.

It is not enough to position yourself only for the characteristics of your product

It is necessary that these are also sought after by the market and that they are not already totally controlled by the competition. In other words, you have to trigger a need and the inability to satisfy it by your competitor. That is how you win in business.

Positioning yourself on the market for a certain category or quality allows you to differentiate yourself from others

The entire content strategy will be defined by always referring to the added value that we guarantee and will aim to associate the brand with that distinctive feature that allows the simplest and most immediate mental association possible for the final consumer.

Market and competition analysis

We know we want to differentiate ourselves, but how can we do it if we do not have full and precise knowledge of what our competitors are doing?

Content strategy is still marketing, and marketing needs a benchmark. A comparative analysis with respect to our direct competitors is essential to trace the differences, their respective weaknesses and strengths. Without forgetting a broader investigation than what other similar companies do but outside our specific market, in order to obtain some useful ideas to integrate our content marketing plan.

Multi-channel content strategy

A multi-channel content strategy is essential. Stories and contents on the internet can branch out expanding, wandering, deepening, even through hypertext links. They can migrate between multiple platforms, channels, also passing from online to offline and vice versa. Our final consumer himself is now multi-channel, therefore multiplying the possibilities of intercepting him can only be one of our primary objectives.

We will have to do this by taking into account that each channel has its own characteristics that define it, peculiarities that must be taken into account already in the strategy definition phase, devising contents that can intercept and engage the audience that uses them.

What works for Facebook will most likely not work for LinkedIn, or Twitter and vice versa. The people reached will be different, the communication model adopted on the different platforms will be different.

Ignoring this aspect and republishing the same content on each different digital channel can only condemn our editorial plan to irrelevance.

Organic share and promoted content

A good web content editor knows he has to follow the guides provided by the content strategist on the creation and dissemination of his contents. It will also be essential, already in the drafting phase of the strategy, to define a budget to be allocated to sponsored content. Entrusting your editorial calendar to organic distribution alone could be very limiting.

Social advertising allows us to define with extreme precision the audience we can hit. Furthermore, knowing right from the start on which categories of content to invest in order to guarantee them the necessary "push" to establish themselves and get closer to our business objectives simplifies and simplifies processes.

Chapter 11 - Content Strategies for Different Buyer Personas

In previous chapters we have discussed the importance of having a good content strategy. We have also touched on the point that there is not a better content in absolute terms, but that it depends on who consumes said content. Let's dive a bit deeper in this concept.

Creating customized content for different buyer personas is essential to engage different consumer or user groups. David Meerman Scott gives the example of the creation of a university site that must address buyer personas with very different characteristics, objectives and motivations. In this case, the site must contain pages with content suited to the needs and expectations of the various interested parties.

Demonstrating how the creation of content can vary within the same site, the expert illustrates five possible buyer personas to be developed: former students, who are contacted to convince them to make donations; high school students, worried about submitting an application for university access and who need clear and detailed information; the parents of prospective students, who will certainly look for reassuring information on where the off-site students will live; current students to be persuaded to enroll again in a master's or other course of study; a more general section with the most frequently asked questions to avoid wasting time in university offices.

Different people come to the site or shop for different reasons, they are used to a different language and expect to find a certain type of information or certain products, which is why marketers, as explained by the expert, should undertake to use the information on buyer personas to create specific marketing and PR plans to reach each one of them.

Chapter 12 - Instagram for Social Media Marketing

The most used social media platform is Instagram and it is the social network we are going to focus on in this book.

On Instagram, companies have the opportunity to meet a community of over 1 billion active users per month and more than 500 million active users every day.

Instagram offers you the opportunity to convince your audience to take a certain action through the creation of visual content, hence visual marketing and recently a new vertical video format that is changing the consumption of content. We are referring to Instagram TV.

Wondering how you can improve your Instagram presence and create an active community around your brand? Here's how to take advantage of all the opportunities.

Instagram users love to connect with your brand

According to Iconosquare, as early as 2015, 62% of Instagram users followed a brand on this platform. Instead, according to a Forrester study, Instagram was found to be offering businesses 58 times more opportunities for success than Facebook and 120 times those of Twitter.

Forrester looked at the top seven social networks, six of which showed that companies manage to achieve a user engagement rate of less than 0.1%. For Instagram, this value reaches 4.21%.

The incredible level of interaction that can be achieved is given by the faithful and active nature of Instagram users.

Building your brand or educating your customers is a central part of any successful business and Instagram plays an extremely important role in this regard.

Instagram's rapid rise continues, detracting from Snapchat and Facebook's stagnant growth rates. This large audience is now a strong draw for IGTV the video hub just launched by Instagram. While IGTV's monetization possibilities are already foreseen in the future, content creators could gain new exposure and build their fan base even stronger.

It is proven that social networks have an increasing influence on users' purchasing decisions, after all that is what social media marketing and this book are all about.

By finding the right mix of relevant content you will have the ability to attract more interest in your brand and push your users without having to invest too much in presentations and expensive marketing activities. In fact, the numbers we just showed you clearly paint a picture where Instagram is the go-to channel for brands and companies that do not have a big budget to spend on social media marketing, as the attention on Instagram is currently undervalued.

Why is Instagram a unique social network? Here are the main reasons.

- It is fully mobile
- It is based on visual design
- It has practically no links

To be successful on Instagram it is not enough to post beautiful images and photos randomly. On the contrary, it is necessary to follow these rules.

- Have a clear vision on goals and strategy
- Publish with a constant frequency
- Be familiar with your followers
- Have a well-defined style guide

By combining all these ingredients, you have the opportunity to reach your audience directly and in a focused way, to increase their interest, increase brand awareness and see impressive results in terms of return on investment.

The first fundamental step in an Instagram marketing strategy is to define the goals you want to achieve. You can apply the SMART method we discussed in chapter 7.

Even if you have never used this platform or you are starting to use it and the results have not arrived yet, it is important that you have specific goals in mind to achieve.

In this way the contents produced can be focused on reaching them and will be more consistent in the eyes of your followers and customers.

Companies usually use Instagram to showcase their product or service, build a community, increase brand awareness, tell the story of the company and its values, increase brand loyalty and share news and updates.

It is very important to choose one or two goals to pursue. We advise you to choose 1 to 2 goals from this list.

- Promote products or services
- Building new relationships
- Show behind the scenes of the company
- Introduce company personnel
- Representing the most informal and fun part of the business

The creative opportunities and visual aspects of Instagram - if you strategically use Stories to show the personality and faces behind your brand - can be especially powerful for highly visual businesses and a great way to creatively engage customers and employees, reach out to your potential customers and build relationships with them.

Once the goals and metrics for evaluating achievable results have been defined, it becomes important to understand which audience you want to target.

The main focus of marketing is to communicate the right message to your audience just when they want to hear it and knowing the demographic characteristics of the user who uses a platform is a central element to understand if you are reaching the target audience or not.

This is why we recommend that you start by immediately defining your buyer persona, as described in previous chapters. We hope you are starting to see how everything is connected together in social media marketing.

Once you have defined the goals and determined the effectiveness of Instagram for your target, you can get to the heart of your strategy following some simple steps.

1. Optimize your profile
2. Create an editorial plan
3. Define the timeline of your posts
4. Measure the returns on your effort

How to optimize your Instagram profile

When someone searches for a keyword on Instagram such as "lighting design", the list of accounts that will be displayed are those that have the keyword in their profile name.

The order or ranking of these accounts will depend on how Instagram determines that they may be of interest to the user researching that term.

If someone you follow follows an account associated with the keyword you enter, Instagram will show you that account and include this information in the list. This immediately gives the user a reason to choose yourself from everyone and build more trust.

Think of your Instagram profile as a homepage.

In your profile you have the possibility to share some information about your company and to insert links to send traffic to your website. So, the real question becomes how you can optimize your Instagram profile.

By making the most of the four elements below you will be able to create high value for your users:

The company biography and description

The description must be closely linked to the brand. What you choose to share in the short space made available by Instagram must be representative of your story, your offer and your values and must be able to explain to users what you do. In addition to this, companies tend to insert a slogan or a tagline as in the case of Nike's "Just Do It". Larger companies can also choose to include their hashtag within the description.

The profile picture

It is very important that your brand is immediately recognizable when a user looks at your post or visits your profile. For most businesses this means using their own logo, a brand (the logo minus some words) or a mascot as their profile picture.

The links

Unlike other social networks, Instagram doesn't allow you to add links to posts. The only part where you can add links is in your profile's personal information. Many companies tend to use this link to bring users to their homepage, however it is also possible to use this possibility to drive traffic to a particular landing page or content. Only available to verified Instagram account holders, there is the option to add links to Instagram Stories as long as you have reached 10,000 followers or more.

Instagram Business Profile

In July, Instagram released the news of the launch of a new tool that is very useful for all companies: the Business Profile.

Currently, this feature is still being tested and is only available in the United States, New Zealand and Australia, but will also be available in other countries in the coming months. With this new tool, companies will have the opportunity to link their Instagram profile to their Facebook page, have insights and statistics on followers and posts and promote targeted posts to achieve pre-established goals directly from their app. In this way you will be able to know which posts are more successful, on which days and in which time slot your target is most active and who your audience is on Instagram. The news does not end there. With this new feature, in fact, users will have the ability to get in touch with the company with a simple touch on the "Contact" button directly from the app.

Optimize your Instagram feed for business

To be successful on Instagram you can't overlook any element so you have to pay attention to how your profile looks as a whole.

Your feed is the first opportunity you have to make a good impression and entice people to hit the "follow" button. And since your Instagram profile is becoming as important as the homepage on your website, you need to make sure it lives up to it.

When someone visits your Instagram profile, they'll decide in seconds whether or not to follow your business by quickly scrolling through your feed, reading your bio, or clicking on the highlights of your stories.

When it comes to converting visitors to followers, it's no longer just the photo editing style that needs to be consistent.

Fortunately, it's easy to create a professional-looking feed with a well-curated and cohesive Instagram aesthetic.

Gorgeous Instagram aesthetic isn't a new trend on Instagram. Companies of all sizes, from startups to super brands, have been curating their feeds to attract new followers for a very long time now.

Your feed doesn't have to adhere to the all-white, with perfect Instagram minimal aesthetic images to be successful, it just needs to be consistent with your brand and target market.

What's important in 2021 is that you make sure every aspect of your feed and every post aligns with the aesthetic you've chosen for your brand.

So whether you're posting to Instagram Stories, posting an IGTV video, or creating profile page highlights, you need to make sure everything lines up and represents your global brand and Instagram aesthetic.

You can plan the look of your Instagram feed and aesthetics using a third-party Instagram marketing platform. Today you have many options available in this regard, just do a quick research online.

Use a good photo editing program or app

When it comes to editing and enhancing your photographs, a reliable photo retouching program with features that can speed up operational time is what you need.

This is a good investment in not only making your Instagram feed good-looking, but also getting more Instagram followers.

Creating a cohesive Instagram feed can be achieved by using the same 1-2 filters or presets on each photo.

This greatly simplifies the merging of all your photos and also reduces editing time.

Chapter 13 - Content Strategy for Instagram

Photo and video content are the heart of Instagram.

The more than 100 million photos and videos shared every day on the platform are proof of this.

But what should the content you post be about?

Before thinking about the visual content, style and design it is useful to define an overview of the message you want to convey and the topics you want to cover. Some companies focus on their product (as does Nike Running, for example), others on community needs and their culture (as WeWork does).

Content is King but Context is Queen, remember that.

In terms of content strategy, on Instagram as for any social network, there is no precise rule to follow. It all depends on the context in which you operate but above all on your buyer persona, or rather, what you might expect to see and interact with your ideal customer.

The important thing is to create content that is able to interest and engage your followers and that allows you to achieve your goals.

For this reason, the starting point must be to build the fundamentals on which to then develop the contents.

All companies, regardless of size, sector or geographic location, have the ability to share quality content on Instagram. This content can relate to the stories of the people who make up the company, the corporate culture, the product and its uses, demonstrations and so on.

The contents most shared by companies are the following.

- Behind the scenes
- User generated content (through re-sharing)
- Product demonstrations and showcases
- Educational contents (guides)
- Cultural contents able to show the ethics and values of the brand
- Fun and entertainment
- Customer stories and case studies
- Team presentation

Before deciding on what type of content to focus on, it may be useful to brainstorm to collect ideas and then formulate the content marketing strategy.

Tell a story

The future of Instagram marketing is all about telling a story with your photos.

As with all content, the quality level continues to rise in social media and brands that want to break through, especially on Instagram, will have to prioritize the great over the simply good, even if it means reducing the frequency of publication.

On Instagram, it helps a lot even if your feed tells the same overall story through notable content and iterations. If your content ranges in many directions, it's very difficult to gain devotees who share a common infatuation with a specific topic.

Instagram is inundated with mediocre messages from brands who forget that the social network is supposed to be a "visual inspiration platform".

Fascinating audiences through images, videos and stories, don't just advertise. This is one of the secrets to having success on Instagram.

Instead, become a storyteller, offer "micro-stories" through captions, videos, Instagram stories and Instagram profiles and thus increase engagement rates.

Authenticity is a winner

In 2020, Instagram did a lot to cleanse the platform of bots, fake likes, fake "influencers", and make malicious services that sell fake followers cease to exist.

Furthermore, Instagram continues to fight not only against automation apps, but also against users who take advantage of them. If you resort to artificial tools that automate your online presence you may see some of your Instagram features removed as a form of "punishment" for using bad practices.

Edelman's 2020 Trust Barometer found that 60% of people no longer trust social media companies. Being able to be perceived as trustworthy is fundamental, so make sure you do everything you can in this regard.

Create authentic content, tell stories with your subtitles and use Instagram Stories features such as emoji, slider, gif or question sticker to increase engagement.

Because of Instagram's algorithm, creating beautiful and engaging content isn't enough to increase your engagement rate.

You need to set up daily routines that will help you get more engagement. Like, comment and interact with your audience or potential followers, don't just go social, be social.

It is vital to commit for at least 10-30 minutes before and after the post is published, plan the posts but also comment, share and create Instagram stories on it.

Here are 3 success stories that showcase the importance of doing what we have just told you.

- The pillars of the Saturday Night Live Instagram profile are behind the scenes of the show and exclusive clips reserved for followers.

- FedEx's Instagram profile focuses on visual content regarding the means used by the company to make its deliveries such as vans, trucks and planes. Their feed is a mix of artistic and exciting photo content.

- Oreo, on the other hand, puts its product at the center through fun and highly engaging content. Often they insert funny phrases within the images and use very colorful and consistent backgrounds to make their posts stand out within the platform.

6 Fundamental Steps for an Effective Instagram Content Plan

Once the themes have been defined (which, however, can always be revised based on the results of the campaigns) it is time to bring them together into an editorial plan.

This way you should be able to define the style and design of your posts and how often you post content.

To have a coherent profile on Instagram and be able to convey the right message, it is important to follow a precise style that reflects that of the other marketing channels used. In this regard it is possible to create real style guides to follow when creating content. These are the points to keep in consideration when doing this process.

- **The composition**. It refers to the positioning of elements within the visual content and, more generally, to the structure of the photo or video. Not all marketers are expert photographers, so it may be useful to define some rules regarding the background, the main focus of the content and the space needed for text at the top or bottom of the image.

- **Color palette**. Always using the same range of colors you have the possibility to create a consistent and focused feed.

Warning! Defining a series of shades to use doesn't mean depriving yourself of the possibility of using other colors, but it will help you give a familiar touch to your content. A good idea is to choose a color range in line with the one usually used by the brand in other marketing channels, in this way users will more easily recognize your company and, consequently, your brand.

- **Font**. If you insert quotes or texts within the images you post on Instagram it is important that you are able to create coherence also through the fonts used that must be in line with the rest of the corporate communication.

- **Filters**. These tools can turn even the photos taken by the most inexperienced photographers into a high quality picture. Filters can drastically change the look of your photos and videos, so it is important to choose to use only some of them (those most in line with your message) in order not to confuse the user. Using a different filter for each post creates confusion and disorientation in your followers who will no longer easily recognize your posts.

- **Caption**. Instagram provides more than adequate space for image descriptions, once this limit is exceeded, the text will be truncated. This space allows you to further differentiate your content and take it to the next level. There are various ways to use this space. Some use it for micro-blogging, others use it to insert a catchy short title or to ask users questions. The possibilities are endless. The important thing is to always make sure to maintain a certain consistency in what you do.

● **Hashtags**. They have become the most used tool on social networks to categorize the content produced and posted. On Instagram, hashtags allow users to discover new content and accounts to follow. If you want to avoid putting too many hashtags in the caption, a good method is to include them in the comments. By analyzing the hashtags most used by your users before choosing the ones that best suit your content, you can ensure that you reach a wider audience.

Hashtags are extremely important. Like emojis, they are much, much more than a fad used by teenagers. They provide a mechanism for users to quickly navigate through topics of interest by grouping posted messages with hyperlinks.

Choosing the best hashtags for your Instagram posts can make a big difference. Make your hashtags too generic - think #christmas or #fashion - and your post will face competition from millions of other competitors. Instead, use a mix of industry-specific trends and hashtags to find the best topic to connect with your targeted followers.

The number of hashtags you use is also crucial. Even though Instagram allows up to a maximum of 30 hashtags per post, a mass of hashtags under the caption risks appearing untargeted and unprofessional. That's why 91% of top brand posts use seven or fewer hashtags to get lots of likes and comments.

What is the right frequency to post on Instagram?

There is a lot to be said about the consistency and frequency of publications on social networks.

The consistency and frequency with which you post content can help your audience understand when to expect new content from your company, and keeping a constant schedule allows you to maximize engagement without taking breaks or lengthening the silence times when they do not see new updates from you.

A Union Metrics study shows that most brands post on Instagram daily with an average of 1.5 posts per day but this number should definitely not be taken as an indicator.

This study also shows that there is no correlation between an increase in posting frequency and a decrease in engagement as companies posting more than two content per day saw no negative returns.

How nice is it to have a community just waiting to hear the next thing you have to say? This is what creates a planned and relevant editorial plan.

Develop content by creating a pipeline of automated messages that are released based on a defined schedule

As if it were a subscription service, this aspect of an effective Instagram strategy becomes fundamental. Routine meets users' expectations and builds trust by fueling their needs.

To generate constant growth, our advice is to post at least two or three contents a day and experiment with an additional post to understand which type of message best suits your reality and the needs of your audience.

To determine the best time to publish, use a service like Iconosquare or the excellent Co-Schedule. Both these tools work pretty well and we cannot recommend them enough.

These powerful tools provide detailed analysis on a wide variety of aspects, including optimization.

When is it the right time to post?

With the recent changes in the algorithm that manages the Instagram feed, timing is one of the elements taken into consideration by the platform to decide what content to show to users. This is why it is important to post in the time intervals in which your target is most present on Instagram to get more engagement.

According to a research conducted by CoSchedule, the best days to increase engagement on Instagram are Mondays and Thursdays between 8am and 9am (EST).

Obviously, this data comes from a wide-ranging research so it may not reflect the habits of your target. For this it is very important to find out the

Instagram habits of your followers using the Statistics function of your Instagram account. This helps you identify when your followers are most active and allows you to plan accordingly, making sure your posts continue to appear at the top of their feed.

Even if you see most of your followers being active on Instagram at a specific time (usually in the morning and in the evening after work), that doesn't mean your posts will perform better during that time. This is due to the increased competition in those time periods which make it harder to reach the top of the feed on your followers accounts.

There's more engagement on Instagram on weekends (22.3%), so it might be worth scheduling some posts for Saturday or Sunday.

Posting during the weekend with the planning offered by third-party solutions is easy, but you need to find time to respond to messages and comments even on Saturdays and Sundays. If you have a personal brand, you should be accustomed to this anyways.

Once the themes, the frequency of publication and the times for posting have been determined, it is useful to draw up an editorial plan in which to report all the content to be posted and the relative timing.

Unfortunately, Instagram does not currently allow you to program posts directly within the platform itself. However, in order to do so additional software such as UNUM, Planoly, OnlyPult, Later, Instapult and TakeOff can be used.

Interact with your followers and drive interactions

You can simply post your own images, but we've found that success comes when you're proactive in the community you are trying to create.

Invite your followers to interact with your content.

A good way to drive engagement is by using interactive content. Interactive content engages your audience more, increases click-throughs, and offers more opportunities to educate and delight your network.

Create any type of action that stimulates user involvement in your content, in order to activate the algorithm that consequently will allow the content itself to reach as many people as possible.

For this purpose, you can use open or closed questions, ask people to answer a survey, or ask yourself about Instagram Stories.

Imagine each of your posts as an opportunity to interact with your followers. Give your fans something to do and watch how the interactions increase like wildfire.

Obviously don't misrepresent this advice, not every post should contain a call to action. Diversification is key in this regard.

It becomes essential instead to understand that you do not have to ask to buy your product every time, give their email or share your page with everyone they know. It is much more subtle what you are asking.

You need to ask your followers for something that makes them feel good about doing it or reaffirm their values or goals. With this method you can get even 300% higher interaction than a simple publication.

Each post is an opportunity to create interactions, increase conversions and interact with your community. Publishing your content must force users to do more than just "digest" a photo. For explosive growth, users need to push themselves to share your content. Every element of your Instagram post should offer the ability to drive interactions and build your network.

Interactive content helps you increase your engagement rate

According to Forrester, Instagram engagement, measured by consumer likes, shares, and comments is 10 times higher than facebook, 54 times higher than pinterest, and 84 times higher than twitter. Do not sleep on this amazing opportunity and integrate Instagram in your social media marketing strategy.

How to measure the results of your Instagram marketing strategy

Tracking your performance and results is essential for any social media marketing strategy you want to implement.

Doing this allows you to understand which content is most interesting to your audience and allows you to optimize your strategy to take steps toward your goal.

By paying the right attention to the growth in the number of followers, likes and comments on your posts you have the opportunity to understand what is actually working (and therefore bringing results) and what needs to be improved.

Measuring the engagement rate on Instagram is very simple: add the number of likes and comments to your post and divide it by the number of followers you had at the time you posted.

If you want to make more accurate measurements, you can choose to use ad hoc measurement software, social media management or social CRM tools capable of tracking performance, monitoring trends, monitoring the use of hashtags, measuring user engagement and managing multiple profiles.

In this regard, the sentiment analysis tools that allow you to detect when users are talking about you and their attitude towards your brand become very useful.

Chapter 14 - Increase Engagement on Instagram

In this chapter we are taking a look at six practical and quick tips to implement for the growth and increase of engagement on Instagram. If you have gone through the other chapters, you should have no doubts about the importance of having an active community.

1. **Leverage the content posted by your users**

Instagram users provide your business with a large number of quality content. Curating the content posted by your users helps you create an active and interactive community and incentivize your audience to share creative content that shows their way of interacting with your product or service and their relationship with your brand.

1. **Leverage the content posted by your employees**

Employee-generated content receives eight times more engagement than company-shared content. Additionally, employee content increases brand awareness by more than 500%. Your business needs to get employees involved in content creation right away. Companies with engaged employees are known to outperform their competitors; engaging employees in content creation can help create a sense of common purpose.

1. **Include people in your posts to increase interaction**

Georgia Tech analyzed more than a million photos on Instagram and found that photos showing real people get 38% more likes and 32% more comments.

1. **GIFs are better than photos**

GIF format is more eye-catching than photo. GIFs are shared more than JPEG or PNG formats, and are more expensive and more effective than producing video. GIFs inspired Instagram to create boomerangs that record a short sequence of still images before combining and scrolling them back and forth, ready to be uploaded to the platform. The tool has already produced excellent results for brands that have pioneered this futuristic means of increasing Instagram engagement.

1. Convert Instagram Followers to Email Subscribers

Email remains the conduit for building truly deep customer relationships. This is why brands strive to convert Instagram followers into email subscribers. First, create a clickable bribe in your Instagram posts depending on your target audience. For example, consider offering a reward, free content, or a discount. Once the audience clicks, make sure your landing page includes a strong call to action linked to an email submission form. Finally, create an email list to effectively engage your new email subscribers so you can start developing more meaningful relationships with them.

1. Share your Instagram posts on Facebook

A Buzzsumo study of over 1 billion posts on Facebook, shared by around 3 million company pages, highlighted how content shared directly from Instagram gets more engagement than those posted directly on Facebook. Promote as much as possible your Instagram channel.

For example, promote your Instagram account on Facebook by making a Facebook ad with a clickable link to your Instagram page. You can also take advantage of Instagram's auto-post and cross-promotional tools. Cross-promotion tools allow you to instantly post from Instagram to Facebook, Twitter, Tumblr, and more, bringing followers together across your social networks.

Remember not to cross-promote all your Instagram posts on other social channels or you risk "cannibalizing" your content, negating the need for followers to visit your Instagram channel in the first place.

Chapter 15 - Instagram Direct and the Rise of the Dark Social

Since 2018 there has been an increase in the use of Instagram Direct which, with the addition of GIFs, videos and lately also audio notes, has transformed from a simple one-to-one vehicle to a solid group chat platform. To date, it appears that people are not only actually using this feature, but that it is even becoming a popular alternative to Messenger and WhatsApp.

Thanks to its features, on Instagram Direct it is always easier to start a private conversation and share or copy and paste links with someone on Instagram. Of course, that includes interacting with businesses as well.

So if you don't have a DM strategy in place, it's time to think about it. DMs can be great for customer support, branding humanization, Instagram audience research, increasing sales and conversions, and so much more.

This phenomenon is called Dark Social. Here is the definition of it.

Dark Social refers to all those communications between the company and the target audience (or between the users themselves) that cannot be measured in terms of likes, shares and comments.

However, using a "dark" customer care you have the opportunity to better understand the sentiment of your audience, as well as to have a direct measure of the level of loyalty of your followers.

You may think that the dark approach is suitable only for small and medium size businesses. Well, in reality, even big corporations can get quality data from the "OTC" interactions they have with their customers.

Chapter 16 - 12 Advanced Tactics to Increase your Sales on Instagram

Doing Instagram marketing isn't that simple. Soft skills and knowledge of some tools are required to get started. But the rapid growth of Instagram is also accompanied by an incredible increase in interactions from users.

In fact, some studies have shown that brands on average get 25% more engagement on Instagram than other social networks. Impressive right?

It means that Instagram is a great place to increase brand awareness but also drive sales. The real million dollar question is: where can you find marketing tactics that really work on Instagram? In this chapter we have collected 12 of the most effective strategies you can apply to turn your company Instagram page into a money making machine.

Tactic #1 - Use advanced influencer marketing

Until a year ago not everyone knew the meaning of the term influencer. Today it has forcefully entered the common language. Social marketers who have had satisfactory approaches with influencers in the past, are now faced with very different scenarios.

Influencer marketing has acquired multiple aspects and has truly become an indispensable component of your marketing strategy.

If you read further you will discover the very advantageous opportunities offered by what we could define as the most humanized and authentic marketing strategy of the moment with the necessary exceptions and clarifications.

Consider that there are more than 60,000 influencers on Instagram covering all vertical markets including fashion, beauty, health and wellness, home decor, nutrition and more.

In order to keep their followers and their branded offerings, expect "authenticity" for 2021, as we have mentioned in the chapter dedicated to this year's trends. The days of overly edited posts and photos and comments with Instagram bots are over, leaving room for more authentic experiences and relationships.

Aligning your brand with influencers who truly love your product and are excited to share with their followers is an ideal way to build an authentic relationship on Instagram, as well as get better engagement and outcome.

Adding Instagram influencer marketing into your overall Instagram strategy can help you increase your brand awareness, grow your follower base, and generate more sales.

Instagram influencer marketing has become increasingly significant these days, allowing marketers to collaborate with leaders, industry experts and push brand messaging to a wider audience.

According to a Nielsen report, 92% of consumers trust the recommendations of individuals (even if they don't know them) more than brands. Using trustworthy, reputable and nice people is a great strategy to use to market your brand.

The future of Instagram marketing will increasingly be about relationships and influencer engagement. Since influencers are considered "independent" personalities, aligning your brand with their authoritative voice can add authenticity to your message.

Algorithms continue to favor people over brands and the challenges of creating authentic and engaging visual content for users, given the competition, make using influencers your assurance to continue being heard on Instagram.

However, selecting the right influencer can be difficult.

Plan an influence strategy that includes a short trial period to see how receptive the network of followers of the influencer specifically selected for your brand is.

You also need to make sure that your influencer is provided with the tools, resources and guidance needed to effectively perform their role, that they work side by side with you on the campaign as a true partner.

New collaboration strategies increase social media impact

2020 saw an interesting trend on Instagram that has begun to redefine how brands collaborate with influencers.

While before, most brands sent products to influencers and expected to see a sponsored post in their feeds and stories, now brands are considering taking influencers on vacation.

The premise is simple. Choose the most influential Instagram influencers with millions of followers, send them to hang out in a luxury hotel, let them try the products, and of course let them post all about them.

In this way, fashion brands like Revolve or Boohoo took small groups of Instagram's most followed influencers on vacation, and benefited from their followers in successful campaigns.

The strategy is to curate and coordinate perfect content, in postcard places for perfect images, but also rough shots that showed the brand from other angles.

The tactic is to prepare an exciting adventure, with Instagrammable meals and other offline experiences, allowing influencers to show how the product or service fits into a perfect lifestyle that influencer followers obviously aspire to. Obviously, you should not neglect to include links for purchase in the content of the influencers.

These types of operations, if well prepared, cost a lot.

The ads created, however, are not short 30-second TV commercials, but a series of posts and stories that leave a much longer impact for the brand. Plus, you can promote your brand hashtag, harness the power of user generated content, and reuse the shots for a campaign.

Collaborate with more authentic influencers and therefore more prodigal also towards the brand

"Authenticity" is another great Instagram marketing "trend" in 2021.

Are the days of Instagram posts with perfect poses, overly edited photos and comments on Instagram bots over, leaving room for authentic experiences and relationships?

2020 saw the rise of a new generation of authenticity-focused Instagram influencers, such as Jenna Kutcher, who garnered over half a million followers in one year, going from 166 to 700k + without ever paying for a single follower.

The influencer marketing industry has exploded thanks to Instagram and global advertising spend for influencers is projected to reach $ 5-10 billion by 2021.

While brands are excited about influencer marketing, regular Instagram users are starting to see beyond perfect, sponsored Instagram posts.

In order to maintain their followers and their partnerships with brands, Instagram influencers are expected to become more personal and authentic in 2020. This includes conversing about sponsored content, with influencers coming to thank their followers for supporting their sponsored posts, and explaining how much of their income comes from their business.

The influencers of 2021 build their success by giving continuous evidence of their greater transparency and authenticity on Instagram, they show that they really consume the products of their sponsoring brands, buy them and repurchase them, even going so far as to exhibit the empty packaging. This simple gesture can represent the new genre of influencers, more trustworthy and authentic, more valuable to brands.

Brands are also beginning to give indications in the sense of authenticity

One of the best ways to create authentic brand partnerships is to think long term. Start thinking about the influencers you work with as brand ambassadors and create longer one-year contracts that include multiple interventions per month.

Aligning your brand with influencers who truly love your product and are excited to share with their followers is an ideal way to build an authentic relationship on Instagram.

Having influencer posts consistent with your brand for an extended period of time not only increases brand appeal, but helps their followers start matching your brand with that influencer, which can lead to better engagement and results.

Micro and nano influencers for the best engagement rates

Bigger isn't always better when it comes to Instagram marketing, a reality that many famous influencers face now as brands start working with micro-influencers (accounts that have fewer than 100,000 followers).

"Nano-influencers" are also on the rise, as brands choose to work with average users, with a 1000 follower base, on sponsored posts and brand campaigns.

Nano-influencers are a secret weapon of social media marketers. Nano-influencers have a following of around 5,000 followers but work in a very specific niche. They represent the typical geek friend, which is appreciated on social media.

Although their following is much smaller than that of a celebrity, their community is more involved with what they post.

Two separate studies by HelloSociety and Markerly found that influencers with a smaller following have a much higher engagement rate than top-tier influencers, and both studies noted a drop in engagement rate as the size of the business audience.

According to a Digiday survey, nano-influencers are able to engage up to 8.7% of their followers, while the engagement rate of famous influencers, who have more than one million followers, is only 1.7%.

Partnering with influencers from smaller accounts is not only cheaper, it can also be more effective.

These types of marketing campaigns with nano-influencer and micro-influencer marketing are set to take off in 2021 as brands take advantage of authenticity and algorithms more.

But in 2021, it's not just influencers who benefit from a smaller and highly engaged audience - micro-brands or micro-brands are also on the rise.

Micro-brands are no different from a small company, there is nothing "small" about them.

Micro-brands on Instagram compete with large retailers and are able to generate millions of dollars in revenue with small teams thanks to the power of their data-driven design and low cost of customer acquisition using social media.

Thanks to the hyper-targeting capabilities of Instagram ads, micro brands are able to design and sell products created for a very specific customer, which they can then target on Instagram. Big brands are starting to take notice of their smaller competitors and respond by creating their own in-house micro brands.

These examples are also helpful in demonstrating that people crave more personalized and targeted content, and this year they will quickly click the "don't follow" button if they aren't resonating with the content on your feed.

If you want to keep Instagram followers in 2021, create targeted content for your ideal customer. Use your Instagram analytics to see which content is resonating the most and that your Instagram follower demographics match those of your customers.

Tactic #2 - Leverage on Instagram to position your brand to the maximum with storytelling

The best way to position a brand is to tell a story that people want to hear, right? And what better way to tell a story using visual content? Our brains are "wired" to understand 60,000 images faster than text. This means it is easier for people to understand the message when using images in your strategy.

Here's where Instagram comes in handy. As you probably know, Instagram is 100% visual, every brand needs a story that differentiates their products from other brands, and Instagram is the best social network for sharing visual content.

By posting images that support any type of storytelling that relates to your brand, you can have a better positioning in your audience's mind.

Tactic #3 - Use hashtags wisely to increase engagement

Twitter may have invented social media hashtags, but Instagram really knew how to exploit them and now creating a hashtag strategy on Instagram offers many results.

Selecting the best hashtags for your Instagram posts can mean the difference between appearing as a top post or sinking to the bottom of the feed without a trace.

Nowadays, Instagram hashtags not only rank content and make it searchable by users, but are an effective way to gain more followers, increase engagement, and broaden brand reach and awareness.

Make your hashtags too generic and your post will face competition from potentially millions of others. Instead, use a mix of industry-specific trends and hashtags to find the best hashtag to connect with your targeted followers.

If you want to harness the potential of the platform to reach huge audiences, increasing the role of hashtags on your Instagram is the way to go.

According to research by Agorapulse, Instagram posts with at least one hashtag got 70% more likes and 392% more comments than those without hashtags.

With the decline in organic reach and the rise in paid impressions, with algorithms being introduced to get brands to pay for exposure, hashtags still represent the best way to organically drive your social marketing campaigns, leveraging on social media posts.

Dig deeper into the hashtag research

Researching hashtags before using them is important, as the more relevant and targeted the hashtags are, the more you increase the chances of reaching a target audience who will interact with your published content.

Use Instagram hashtags in a targeted manner

There are many studies on how many hashtags to use in each post to increase engagement. Depending on which study you rely on, the best number of hashtags is between five and the maximum allowed number of 30.

An analysis by TrackMaven found that using 11 hashtags in each post is optimal for increasing engagement on Instagram.

The reality is that the key to Instagram hashtag success is to use them strategically, regardless of whether you decide on three deeply researched or 30 carefully chosen hashtags. You have to be as specific as possible with the hashtags it also limits the targeted user pool, which makes it easier to build a highly engaged audience.

Add hashtags to your Instagram profile bio for conversations and shares

Since the Instagram bio only allows for a standard hyperlink, adding hashtags encourages people to start conversations and share experiences around your brand.

Instagram hashtags can now be inserted into profiles, a feature that provides an extra boost by providing a link to the hashtag feed, however, don't expect to make your bio detectable in the hashtag search results.

Enter "#" before each word in your profile and it will automatically become a clickable link that can be used for anything like promoting the Instagram community you are creating.

Use special daily hashtags to engage and inspire your content

Daily hashtags offer a way to engage with your audience every day, keeping them constantly engaged with your content and connecting with them over the long haul.

Use a balanced combination of general, niche, and location-based hashtags.

Include a brand hashtag in every Instagram post. Use a hashtag for the campaign.

Insert hashtags in Instagram Stories to attract new audiences

Adding hashtags to Instagram Stories - in text, a sticker or a location tag - gives your content another way to be found by new audiences.

But inserting hashtags in images or videos of Instagram stories does not guarantee to reach large slices of new audiences because it all depends on the quality of the content published and their level of engagement.

Organize or join a live event, whether it's a conference, event or vacation, this is the time when people are most engaging in seeing what's happening in real time on Instagram. So making your story visible to others is a great way to get new eyes on your Instagram profile and get more followers.

When your story is added to the location story, you usually get a notification from Instagram. When a photo or video of your story is visible on a hashtag or location page, you will see the name of that page when you look at who has seen your story.

If you go to your Instagram explorer page, you will see the live story for the current city you are in, but your story only has the option to be inserted if you add a location sticker to your Instagram Stories.

Tactic #4 - Cross promotion to grow your followers faster

Most users and brands don't, but cross-promotion (or just co-marketing) is one of the most effective ways to grow your following on any social network.

You can ask one of your stakeholders to tell their followers about you and to follow you, so you can do the same thing with them.

The problem is that initially this practice had become practically spam but now the situation has certainly changed and when co-marketing of this type is carried out with elegance, it can be truly effective.

The biggest mistake when it comes to cross-promotion is sending requests to the wrong people. In order not to waste time, it is very effective to exchange a few messages before starting a real launch, making sure you are natural with a direct and clear message.

We cannot forget Instagram Pods

In recent years, the fashion of Instagram Pods has exploded, also known as Instagram Engagement Pods, i.e. groups (public or private) in which users try to trick the Instagram algorithm to get more followers, likes, comments and views.

The goal of these groups is to increase the engagement of their Instagram profile from real and active users by exchanging likes on posts, and possibly leaving a comment.

There are several ways to access Instagram Pods. Some being public do not need specific rules, others being private, however, require an invitation from one of the members of the group.

The benefits are certainly immediate. The increase in engagement is quick, just take the time to "like" everyone on the pod, hoping they will return the favor.

The disadvantages?

Obviously this practice is not without its pitfalls. First of all, the engagement rate could be staggered, and it could even decrease rapidly if it is not practiced continuously.

So consider all the pros and cons that this would entail and then decide if Instagram Pods groups are right for you to grow on Instagram. Generally speaking, we find this to be a bad idea for everyone that is serious about building a community of potential customers.

Tactic #5 - Use Bridge Marketing to increase sales

Have you ever heard of "Bridge Marketing"? It's when you build a bridge between your business and a specific niche so that more people can feel drawn to your products or services.

For example, let's say that you are starting a company in the sector of industrial lighting and you are looking for specialized designers with whom to start a partnership.

While this type of user is browsing, he may come across an "ad" on Instagram promoting the following message.

"We specialize in industrial lighting, find out more here".

This is nothing more than making sure you segment Instagram Advertising campaigns and create personalized ads for each segment.

As with Facebook, the more specific the segments you are going to create (thanks to the segmentation based on Gender, Place, Age, Niche) and the more useful messages to your audience you can take advantage of.

Tactic #6 - Use videos to communicate the message behind your brand

Most brands have now adopted video marketing, and the frequency of video posts on Instagram has gradually increased over the past few years.

Video marketing on Instagram is the opportunity for a company to show the world who they are and what they do in a minute or less.

People want connections, relationship personalization has pushed to come face to face with your followers, whether it's Instagram stories, Instagram tv or a good old video post.

One of the principle of the moment is: explore the full range of Instagram video formats.

A picture may be worth a thousand words, but a video is worth millions. There is no comparison with the effectiveness and popularity of online video content.

Instagram recognizes this and offers a suite of video options that greatly entice marketers.

For example, consider Instagram Stories "live video" option to reveal new products or services or use a pre-recorded ad to deliver authentic behind-the-scenes stories to your followers to communicate the brand and increase engagement on Instagram.

Less refined videos work best on Instagram Stories

For a long time, brands have been posting very sophisticated videos on Instagram to attract customers. These videos require time and financial commitment to be produced and with the Instagram algorithm it is not possible to grasp the results of the dawn of the platform.

Today, however, less refined but genuine videos, which cost less time to create and publish, work best on Instagram. Instagram users, for the most part, are not interested in watching highly polished videos, preferences have changed over time, but they are looking for content that is authentic and relevant to them.

Invite your employees and managers to talk freely on video about their challenges, in order to promote your company culture. This tactic works incredibly well to increase engagement.

Tactic #7 - Use analytics tools to identify content that generates the most interaction

One of the biggest mistakes people make when managing social media is posting content they "think" will be of interest. Yes, sometimes you can get a fluke and people react very positively to the content, but most of the time this doesn't work.

It is much more effective to share photos or videos that have a proven record of success.

Tactic #8 - Start on Instagram and finish on Facebook

If there are still few people promoting certain products or services on Instagram, it means that there are still huge opportunities available.

An example? Iconic, an Australian fashion and footwear eCommerce, after launching an Instagram campaign to raise awareness of their brand among Australian women and boost sales of new collections, launched a Facebook campaign that targeted the same interests the following week.

The results? Women who viewed the campaign on both Instagram and Facebook converted 23% more than other active campaigns.

Instagram campaigns have increased brand awareness and increased purchase intent while direct ads to the Facebook website prompted people to complete the purchase.

In summary? Launching visually compelling campaigns on Instagram to increase brand awareness, then continuing the campaign via direct ads to increase sales via Facebook is a great way to get the most out of your advertising efforts.

As you can see, Instagram can be an extremely interesting tool that can generate sales when you know how to use it correctly.

Tactic #9 - Guide users through the conversion funnel

For most brands, getting a large number of followers is important but turns out to be just one step in the funnel of global marketing activities.

To move users further down the conversion funnel, any way to capture your followers' email should be considered. And one of the best ways to capture these emails is to ask for it in exchange for something.

Share an image with a call to action and insert a link in the caption on how to download an eBook or subscribe to your newsletter.

Once the user is engaged in this way, it will be possible to proceed step by step to a complete conversion, continuing in another way (through marketing automation actions or one-to-one relationship marketing actions).

To do this, however, it is necessary to create a targeted and tailored landing page. From there it will then be possible to push users through your different channels and keep them updated with your products or services.

Tactic # 10- Mix videos and photos

One of the hottest trends in Instagram marketing is to mix photos and videos in your strategy.

Considering that a video can generate three times more shares than posts made of images only, video is a valuable tool that can be used to engage followers and grow your following and thus the traffic to your website.

For example, take a look at Oreo or McDonald's on Instagram and you'll see impressive examples of stop motion videos using a product to generate ironic and often incredible storytelling.

Videos can be fun, shareable and engaging, and with Instagram's video editing features, great results can be achieved with ease.

In stop motion, for example, simply hold down the Record button and pause when you want to shoot a different scene. Or you can simply upload a pre-recorded video.

Tactic #11 - Host contests on Instagram

Contests are a powerful engagement tool on Instagram, generating 3.5x more engagement and 64x more comments than regular posts.

Despite this, they are regularly neglected by brands: only 2% of them organize contests. This means there is a huge, relatively untapped resource for marketers to leverage.

Organizing a contest on Instagram obviously requires planning a strategy, defining goals and rules and creating posts that attract attention.

The most frequent are the "Repost" contests where, in case of victory, the prize consists precisely in the repost of the winning profile on the social media and other web channels of the promoter of the competition, in this case leveraging people's visibility and ego. Or you can also opt for contests that offer cash prizes or similar: we have already talked about weekends in luxury hotels or shopping vouchers and they make up for a great prize for a contest.

Tactic #12 - Shopping on Instagram

If you run an e-commerce business, you cannot fail to take advantage of one of the new features available on Instagram: the shopping function. This feature allows you to insert tags in your posts and this for followers means to "tap" on the image to see all the information useful for purchasing a product such as the price, the name of the article and the link that refers to the e-commerce page.

The new feature like Shopping in Stories this year has helped advertisers place the shopping bag icon on whatever product or service they are promoting.

With this option, marketers have the ability to target their audience to click on the shopping bag icon and view the product image, information and website link to purchase the product. With over 400 million users using Instagram Stories on a daily basis, advertisers can take advantage of this marketing feature to connect with their target customers.

The idea that users can go from inspiration to action with the click of a button and buy directly without leaving the Instagram app is a winning opportunity for brands, for Instagram, and for shoppers. Please, make sure to include this tool in your social media marketing strategy, as it is a very important one.

For now, only about 20% of marketers actively use shoppable posts, with a vast majority admitting they haven't yet noticed an increase in sales from shoppable tags.

However, shoppability remains an Instagram trending goal, as over 50% of Instagram marketers plan to use more shoppable posts in 2021.

The future of marketing is on Instagram since many Instagram users follow popular brands on this platform (around 80% of users follow at least one brand on Instagram)

Instagram seems to have taken up the challenge of becoming one of the cornerstones of the online shopping experience, with brands and retailers that can use the shopping features to allow followers to purchase items directly on the platform.

There are many elements that can lead you to this important strategic conclusion.

Instagram is focusing more and more on brands also with the introduction of more in-depth data analysis, useful for companies to regulate their activities in the adoption of purchasing functions on the platform.

Shopify, which has more than 500,000 merchants, is helping online retailers expand their offerings on Instagram's shopping features.

Since 2019, Instagram allows you to buy not only from feed posts and stories, but also from explorer posts and videos. Also, Instagram allows you to have your own "Shopping" collection for easy browsing.

Instagram shopping features will be an important part of the platform in 2021. So find the easiest way for your brand to leverage direct-to-consumer sales as part of your overall Instagram marketing strategy.

Conclusion

Congratulations on making it to the very end of this book, it has been a great journey.

We hope you were able to find valuable information to improve the online presence of your company or personal brand using the power of Instagram marketing. We have tried our best to give you every tool and strategy you might need to turn your Instagram page into a money making machine.

Now it is on you to put in practice what you have learned. Because remember that understanding a concept and making it work for you are two totally different things and as an entrepreneur or influencer you should always be willing to take the risk to try and test new strategies.

We are sure that if you commit to seriously working on your Instagram marketing strategy, you will be well ahead of competition. After all, it is not a secret that most businesses have a superficial approach when it comes to their online presence, especially on Instagram. Doing things differently will certainly put you miles ahead of them and will give you an unfair advantage in the long run.

We hope you enjoyed this book and we wish you great success!

Lightning Source UK Ltd.
Milton Keynes UK
UKHW010336301121
394802UK00001B/11